From Crying Baby to Contented Baby

Gina Ford

Vermilion
LONDON

1 3 5 7 9 10 8 6 4 2

Published in 2010 by Vermilion, an imprint of Ebury Publishing
Ebury Publishing is a Random House Group company

The Random House Group Limited Reg. No. 954009

Addresses for companies within the Random House Group can be found at
www.rbooks.co.uk

A CIP catalogue record for this book is available from the British Library

The Random House Group Limited supports The Forest Stewardship
Council (FSC), the leading international forest certification organisation. All our
titles that are printed on Greenpeace approved FSC certified paper carry the FSC logo.
Our paper procurement policy can be found at www.rbooks.co.uk/environment

Mixed Sources

Product group from well-managed
forests and other controlled sources
www.fsc.org Cert no. TT-COC-2139
© 1996 Forest Stewardship Council

Printed and bound in Great Britain by CPI Mackays, Chatham, ME5 8TD

ISBN 9780091929596

To buy books by your favourite authors and register for offers, visit www.rbooks.co.uk

The information in this book has been compiled by way of general guidance in relation to the
specific subjects addressed, but is not a substitute and not to be relied on for medical, healthcare,
pharmaceutical or other professional advice on specific circumstances and in specific locations.
Please consult your GP before changing, stopping or starting any medical treatment. So far as the
author is aware the information given is correct and up to date as at November 2009. Practice, laws
and regulations all change, and the reader should obtain up to date professional advice on any such
issues. The author and publishers disclaim, as far as the law allows, any liability arising directly
or indirectly from the use, or misuse, of the information contained in this book.

Contents

Acknowledgements

I would like to express my thanks and gratitude to the thousands of parents whom I have worked with or advised over the years. Their constant feedback, opinions and suggestions have been an enormous help in writing my books.

I would also like to thank my publisher Fiona MacIntyre and editor Julia Kellaway for their constant encouragement and faith in my work, and a special thank you to Cindy Chan for all her hard work on the final manuscript. Thanks also, as always, to the rest of the team at Vermilion.

Special thanks are also owed to my agent Emma Kirby for her dedication and support and to Kate Brian, the website editor of Contentedbaby.com, for her efforts in gathering information for the book. Thank you to Yamini Franzini, Laura Simmons, Jane Waygood and Rory Jenkins, and the rest of the team at Contentedbaby.com, for their support while I was writing this book and their wonderful work on the website.

And, finally, I am ever grateful for the huge support I receive from the thousands of readers of my books who take the time to contact me – a huge thank you to you all and much love to your contented babies.

Introduction

Since writing my first book *The Contented Little Baby Book* I have received letters and calls from thousands of parents who have told me how much my methods have helped them when they have been at breaking point. Of course, my approach might not suit everyone, but I know it can help relieve the stress and confusion of early parenthood, and has done so for many mothers and fathers.

One of the most stressful things any parent has to endure is to listen to their baby crying, particularly if the crying goes on for any length of time and all attempts to calm the baby fail. In this book I give concise advice on learning the signs of hunger, tiredness, boredom or indeed many of the other reasons that cause young babies to get upset, and I offer effective methods for calming and settling. The fact that you are able to understand his needs and meet them quickly and confidently will leave both you and your baby calm and reassured, and avoid unnecessary crying. From extensive experience, I know that all babies are different and what works with one baby may not work for another. For this reason, my advice in this book can be adapted to suit the individual needs of each baby.

I am confident that this book will teach you how to swiftly recognise why your baby is upset and meet his needs accordingly so you have a calm and contented baby. Being a parent should be a happy and deeply satisfying experience. My advice has worked for many thousands of parents and their contented babies, and they can work for you too.

1
Hunger

Hunger is one of the most common reasons for babies to be unhappy or unsettled, and it is also one of the easiest problems to solve. I always advise parents to assume that their baby is hungry if he is crying, and only start working their way through any other potential causes once they have eliminated hunger as a possibility. Hunger is not only an issue for a new baby when you are establishing feeding, but can cause problems throughout the first year as your baby grows rapidly and his nutritional needs change.

Hunger in the first two months

Feed times: 7am, 10am/11am, 2pm/2.30pm, 5pm, 6pm/6.15pm, 10pm/11pm (plus any middle-of-the-night feeds necessary)

Nap times between 7am and 7pm: 8.30/9am–10am, 11.30am/12pm–2.30pm, 3.30/4.30pm–5pm
Maximum daily sleep: 3½–5½ hours

(These times are only meant as a guide. Adjust the times to suit your baby's individual needs.)

Hunger is a common cause of crying in very young babies, both breast- and bottle-fed, until regular feeding patterns are established. Newborn babies feed frequently and will need a minimum of eight feeds a day. In the very early days some babies may need even more. Frequent feeding is important in helping to stimulate your milk supply. Hunger can become an issue when babies go through a growth spurt around the third week when their appetitie increases and they need more milk.

Breast-fed babies

In my experience of working personally with hundreds of mothers, getting off to the best start with breast-feeding in the very early days can help avoid hours of endless crying in the early months. In all of my books I say that I do not agree with the term 'demand feeding', but this does not mean that I advise a baby should not be fed when he is hungry. The reason I am opposed to this term is that, all too often, newborn babies are so sleepy that they do not demand to be fed. These long intervals between feeds in that important first week can often mean a mother's breasts are not being stimulated enough, and by the second or third week can result in a baby becoming very irritable and crying excessively on and off for hours through genuine hunger because the mother is not producing enough milk.

For this reason, I advise that from the very beginning newborn babies are woken and fed every three hours. This time is calculated from the beginning of one feed to the beginning of the next feed. I do also stress that should a baby be crying before the end of three hours, then of course the baby **must be fed.**

If your baby suddenly becomes more unsettled around the third week, which is usually around the time of the first growth spurt, you may find your baby demanding to be fed on and off around the clock. It is very possible that you are not producing enough milk, particularly if he has not yet regained his birth weight. When this happens, I would suggest that for a couple of days you express 15–30ml (½–1oz) from each breast **before** you feed your baby. The reason I say to express before feeds is that your baby will always be more efficient about extracting milk (especially the hind milk) from the breast than an expressing pump will be. For the first couple of days you may find that your baby will need to feed even more often, but this will quickly help you increase your milk supply.

The milk that you express during the day can be used to top-up after the 6.15pm and 10pm feeds, which will help your baby go slightly longer in the night.

When this longer spell happens you should feel your breasts become slightly more engorged which is a sign that you are producing more milk. You can then increase the amount you express at the 7am and 10am feeds to 30ml (1oz) from each breast. After a week or so, you should notice your baby is happy to go slightly longer between feeds, and he may even need less milk at the top-up feeds. However, to ensure that you do not end up with a very unsettled baby during the next growth spurt at around six weeks, I would recommend that you continue to express at least 60–90ml (2–3oz) at the 7am feed, and at least 30–60ml (1–2oz) at the 10am feed.

During the first couple of months expressing in the morning will mean that when your baby goes through a growth spurt, you can simply decrease the amount you express which results in your baby receiving the extra milk he needs, avoiding any excessive crying spells due to hunger in the early days. For further more in-depth information on low milk supply please see *The New Contented Little Baby Book*.

✿ Breast-fed babies may cry from hunger if they are not getting sufficient quantities of hind milk. It can take up to 25 minutes feeding on the first breast for them to get beyond the fore milk and reach the hind milk. Hind milk has a much higher fat content than the fore milk. If they are moved too quickly to the second breast, they may get insufficient hind milk and become hungry again sooner.

✿ If a baby is continually crying and unhappy, he may not have latched on to the breast properly. Mothers are often discharged from hospital before they can confidently latch their baby on to the breast, a technique that is essential to successful breast-feeding. It is important to seek advice from your midwife or breast-feeding counsellor. If he is not latched on properly, a baby can seem to be constantly sucking for up to an hour at a time, without getting sufficient milk. I always advise that mothers whose breast-fed babies can't go happily for two or three hours between feeds should seek advice from an experienced breast-feeding counsellor.

Bottle-fed babies

❀ Parents often assume that feeding will be far more straight-forward with a formula-fed baby and that problems are unlikely to arise. Of course, it is true that you will be able to see how much formula your baby takes at each feed, but hunger can still cause problems. A formula-fed baby needs approximately 75–90ml (2½–3oz) of milk for each pound of his body weight each day, divided by the number of feeds he is having.

❀ Some parents are tempted to try to restrict their formula-fed baby's feed in the middle of the night in an attempt to get him to sleep through, but this can lead to the baby waking up and crying a couple of hours later through genuine hunger. If you ensure your baby feeds enough in the middle of the night to get him through to the morning, he is more likely to sleep longer and you are less likely to have a crying baby at night.

✿ Some bottle-fed babies drink their formula very quickly, and I believe this could prevent their natural sucking instincts from being met. If your baby often screams when you take the bottle out of his mouth after drinking the right amount of formula for his weight, this could be the cause of the problem rather than hunger. Try using a slower flowing teat and offering a dummy after the feed. If your baby continues to get upset it is possible that he may need bigger feeds. Before increasing the recommended amount for your baby's weight, always consult your doctor or health visitor.

Case study: George, aged four weeks
Problem: Formula-fed baby waking up screaming during the night

I was contacted by George's parents when he was four weeks old. He weighed more than 4.5kg (10lb) and had been feeding at 3am and 7am. They were concerned that he seemed to have suddenly back-tracked, waking up screaming and wanting to be fed at 2am and 6am.

I asked how much milk George was taking in his last feed at 10pm, and was told that he would not take more than 90–120ml (3–4oz). A formula-fed baby of this weight would usually be taking around 120–150ml (4–5oz) at the last feed. As he was taking less than the amount suggested, I suspected he had started to wake up because he was genuinely hungry.

I advised George's parents to try giving him a split feed, the first part at 10pm and then the second at 11pm to increase the amount of milk he took. This, along with having him awake for a good hour and a quarter more, would possibly be enough to help him sleep for a longer stretch in the night.

For George, this did make all the difference – keeping him awake for a while and giving him more formula meant that he started sleeping for longer. I was aware that at this age he was likely to be going through a growth spurt, and he could simply be hungry and need feeding more often. In the circumstances, if the split feed hadn't been enough, I would have advised feeding him at 2am and 6am. He would still be doing very well for a four-week-old baby. The above advice would also work well with a breast-fed baby who starts waking earlier in the middle of the night.

Hunger at three to four months

Feed times: 7am, 11am, 2.15/2.30pm, 6.15pm, 10/10.30pm (plus any middle-of-the-night feeds necessary)

Nap times between 7am and 7pm: 9am–9.45am, 12pm–2/2.15pm
Maximum daily sleep: 3 hours

(These times are only meant as a guide. Adjust the times to suit your baby's individual needs.)

By the time your baby reaches this age, you will probably have established a routine and feeding patterns and be feeling more confident about interpreting your baby's cries. If you have been following the *Contented Little Baby* routines, I hope they will have helped you to pre-empt your baby's feeding needs, too. However, hunger can still cause problems at this age, particularly with a breast-fed baby where a low milk supply at certain times of the day can leave your baby hungry and lead to crying.

* If your breast-fed baby is under four months, crying exces-sively in the evening and gaining less than 180g (6oz) each week, you may have a low milk supply in the evening. I recommend expressing 60ml (2oz) in the first two morning feeds in order to increase milk supply. This expressed milk can also be used to top up a feed in the evening.

* If your baby is waking up crying two or three times in the night, don't assume it is because he is ready to take solids. His hunger is more likely to be due to him not getting full milk feeds during the day or not having enough feeds during the day.

* Breast-fed babies may continue to need middle-of-the-night feeds for longer than a formulated baby.

✿ A totally breast-fed baby will still need a late feed and perhaps an early morning feed at around 5–6am until he starts to take solids at around six months.

✿ If your baby suddenly starts waking up crying earlier than usual, whether he is breast- or bottle-fed, I suggest that you try introducing a split feed at 10/11.15pm for at least a week, making sure your baby is fully awake at that time. If you are breast-feeding, it would also be worth offering both breasts at 10pm, then a top-up of expressed milk at 11.15pm. If your baby does not take more at this split feed, you could try introducing a split feed at 5/6.15pm, as having more milk at 5pm should help to increase his appetite for the split late feed. If you find that your baby starts to sleep later in the morning, I suggest continuing this for another week and then you can start to reduce the time he is awake, slowly bringing the 11.15pm feed back towards 10pm. If he continues to sleep through to close to 7am from the 10pm feed, you can reduce the time he is awake until it becomes a sleepy feed.

This may mean your baby will only take a very small top-up feed at 7.30/8am and need to feed again at around 10am, with a top-up just before his lunchtime nap, to ensure that he sleeps well. If you follow this advice for at least a week, and your baby is still crying and unsettled in the middle of the night, then it is worth dropping the 10pm feed for a short period to see exactly how long he will sleep for if left to waken naturally. If he sleeps to around 1am, takes a full feed then and then sleeps until 7am, it would be worth following this plan for at least a week. Once your baby has got used to sleeping for a longer spell in the night, you can reintroduce the 10pm feed, in the hope that he will start to sleep until nearer 7am.

❀ Sometimes it is still necessary to give a baby of this age more frequent, smaller feeds. Although giving so many smaller feeds is not ideal, I believe it is better than leaving a baby to cry or become unsettled for lengthy periods at 5/6am. If leaving your baby to settle himself back to sleep at this time is going to work, it will do so within a matter of days, but continuing to leave a baby unsettled at this time is, in my experience, why some parents end up with a long-term early waking problem.

Case study: Arun, aged 15 weeks
Problem: Unsettled and crying on and off between 5am and 7am

Arun's parents started the Contented Little Baby *routines when he was three weeks old. Within just a week he was sleeping his longest spell from the late feed, and by nine weeks he was sleeping regularly to 7am. Then suddenly, at around 12 weeks, he started to wake up anywhere between 5am and 6am. Initially, he would go back to sleep after a quick cuddle, but it soon became harder to settle him. His parents were convinced he was not waking due to hunger and tried settling him with* cooled boiled water, but things got worse and by 15 weeks he was waking at 5am and would cry on and off until they got him up at 7am. Because he was not sleeping well between 5am and 7am, he also started to become more unsettled during the day, crying and fussing after being awake only an hour and needing to go down much earlier than usual for his naps.

He continued to settle well between 7pm and 10pm, but he would only ever take one breast at the late feed. By the time he was 15 weeks, things had got so bad that his parents contacted me. Although they were not convinced, I felt that genuine hunger was most likely to be the initial cause of Arun waking and crying at 5am. Because he had got so used to being awake at that time, he had also become overtired during the day and started to need more sleep. This increased daytime sleep created a vicious circle of him needing more sleep *because he was awake so much in the night, and he was continuing to wake in the night because he was having too much sleep during the day.*

In order to resolve the problem I advised his parents to try and increase the amount he took at his late feed, so that he slept longer in the night. Once he was sleeping better in the night, we could then reduce the amount of daytime sleep he was having.

The first thing I advised his parents to do was to go back to offering a split feed at 5/6.15pm, so that he would take more at a second split feed at 10/11.15pm. I felt that as he weighed well over 6kg (14lb), just having one breast at the late feed was not enough to get him sleeping through to 7am. I also advised that when he woke at 5am, it was vital that he should be fed right away so that he settled quickly, and slept until closer to 7am.

His parents followed this advice for a week, but Arun would never take the second breast and continued to wake at 5am, at which time his mother would feed him. Sometimes he would settle back to sleep well until 7am, but at other times he would be unsettled.

At this stage, I suggested that his parents should go back to offering Arun a full feed after his bath, and not wake him for the late feed. Instead, they should allow him to wake up naturally, in the hope that if he slept longer he would then take a feed from both breasts when he woke. The first night he woke just after midnight and got sleepy after feeding from one breast, but, as I advised, his mother turned up the light slightly and changed his nappy to wake him so that he would take the other breast. He fed for a further 20 minutes on the second breast, then settled well and slept until just after 6am.

He fed well, but did not go back to sleep and then was tired by 8am. In the past his parents had been letting him sleep from 8am to nearer 10am, as he was so tired from his unsettled spell between 5am and 7am.

To reduce his daytime sleep but avoid him becoming overtired I advised that his parents should try a split morning nap, allowing 15/20 minutes at 8am, and then another 15/20 minutes at 9.30/10am. This split nap would reduce his morning sleep by over an hour, but also avoid him becoming overtired.

Within a couple of weeks Arun was sleeping from 7pm to around 3/3.30am at which stage he would feed well from both breasts and sleep soundly until 7am. Now that Arun was used to going a longer stretch in the night, I suggested seeing if he would go the eight hours from the late feed to 7am.

I advised his parents to reintroduce the split feed

again at 5/6.15pm to ensure that he was hungry at the late feed. I also suggested that for a week or so they let Arun sleep until nearer 11pm to ensure that he took a good feed from both breasts.

The first week he fed and settled well at around midnight and slept through to nearer 7am. The following week I suggested that his parents start to gradually bring forward the 11pm feed to 10pm. They should wake Arun up no later than 10.45pm for the next three nights, and if he fed and slept until nearer 7am, they could then bring the time forward to 10.30pm. They continued to bring the late feed forward by 10 minutes until he was feeding at 10pm. I also suggested that as Arun was totally breast-fed, it would be best to keep the 5/6.15pm split feed in place to ensure he fed from both breasts at the 10pm feed. Cutting down the number of breast-feeds or the length of breast-feeds a baby has too quickly *can result in a reduction in a mother's milk supply which in turn lead to a baby who was sleeping well starting to wake up in the night again genuinely hungry.*

I advised that should Arun start to wake up again between 5am and 7am, and not settle back to sleep quickly, they should always assume that hunger is the cause and feed him back to sleep quickly, so that he does not get into the habit of being unsettled for lengthy periods at that time of the night.

Hunger at five to six months

Feed times: 7am, 11am, 2.15/2.30pm, 6.15pm, 10pm
(plus any middle-of-the-night feeds necessary)

Nap times between 7am and 7pm: 9am–9.45am,
12pm–2/2.15pm
Maximum daily sleep: 2½–3 hours

*(These times are only meant as a guide. Adjust the
times to suit your baby's individual needs.)*

At this age, feeding is well established but your baby will
continue to go through growth spurts, and hunger can be a
common cause of crying as his nutritional needs change. The
current guidelines state that solids should now be introduced
at six months, rather than at four months as previously recommended. Your baby will need more milk during this additional
two-month period. In my experience, five milk feeds a day

may not be sufficient. Some babies may need to go back to having a milk feed in the night or early morning until solids are introduced around six months.

* If you decide to drop the 10pm feed and your baby starts to wake earlier and not settle back to sleep quickly, then you should assume that it is due to hunger and feed him. It would then be worth considering re-introducing the 10pm feed, until solids are established.

* In the early months, babies usually go through a growth spurt every three weeks. During growth spurts you may find that your baby is not content on five feeds a day, and you may have to offer a split feed in the morning, and also re-introduce the 5pm feed.

* If your baby becomes very discontented between feeds, despite being offered extra milk, and you think that he is showing signs of needing to be weaned (see below), then it is important to discuss this with your health visitor or doctor before taking any action.

A baby could be ready to be weaned if:

* He has been taking a full feed four or five times a day and has been happily going for four hours between feeds, but now gets irritable and chews his hands long before his next feed is due.

* He has been taking a full feed and then screaming for more the minute the feed finishes.

* He usually sleeps well at night and at nap times but is starting to wake up earlier and earlier.

* He is chewing his hands excessively, displaying eye-to-hand co-ordination and trying to put things in his mouth.

Hunger at six to nine months

Feed times: 7am, 11.45am, 2.30pm, 5pm, 6.30pm, (10.30pm) (plus any middle-of-the-night feeds necessary)

Nap times between 7am and 7pm: 9.15/9.30am–9.45/10am, 12.30pm–2.30pm
Maximum daily sleep: 2½–2¾ hours

(These times are only meant as a guide. Adjust the times to suit your baby's individual needs.)

Guidelines recommend that babies are weaned at six months. At this stage, as you work towards establishing a balanced diet with three meals a day, hunger can still be a cause of crying.

* If you started weaning your baby on to solids at six months, he will probably continue to need a small milk feed at 10pm until he is around seven months old.

* If a breast-fed baby is weaned at six months, it is important that iron-containing foods, such as breakfast cereals, broccoli, lentils and baby food fortified with iron are introduced swiftly. You will need to progress quickly through the food groups to include meat or vegetarian alternatives for their iron content. Babies on formula will have their iron supplemented in the milk.

* By seven months, your baby should be having protein foods rich in iron at lunchtime, as he will have used up all the iron stored in his body when he was born. Babies rely on the introduction of iron-containing foods.

* Some babies who are still drinking large amounts of milk at six months may be resistant to the introduction of solids. If you find that your baby is fussy about taking solids, you should only offer him half his milk at the 11am feed to

encourage interest in the solid food. If this does not improve his appetite then I would advise offering solids first, followed by the milk.

✿ By the seventh month, most babies are on their way to being established on three solid meals a day. Once this happens, they should need no more than three to four milk feeds a day. This will give all the milk needed for your baby's nutritional needs. If you continue to feed your baby in the night, he will not increase his solids at the rate needed. Between six and nine months, some babies who had previously slept well may start to wake up crying in the night because they are not taking the right amount of solids for their age and weight. Once your baby is taking three solid meals a day, he should manage to sleep from 7pm to 7am.

Case study: David, aged seven months
Problem: Excessive night-time feeding

When David outgrew his Moses basket at five months of age, his parents decided that they would move his 20-month-old sister Andrea into a bed and give her cot to David. He continued to sleep well when moved to the big cot, but the move to a bed for Andrea turned out to be a disaster and resulted in weeks of hysterical crying and sleepless nights.

While the situation with Andrea was becoming steadily worse, exhaustion led David's mother to start giving jars of baby food rather than the fresh food that had been an essential part of his dietary requirements. She also started to cut out his bath and massage in the evening. Soon David started to wake up every night at around 10pm and would not settle back without a feed, even though he had dropped this feed a good six weeks previously. Worse still, he started to wake up when his sister was crying in the night. His mother ended up giving him a formula feed in the night so that he would settle back quickly and allow her to return to a hysterical Andrea.

This excessive night-time feeding resulted in David becoming overtired during the day, causing him to be fussy at mealtimes. He would take only a small amount of cereal after his morning bottle, about two tablespoonfuls of vegetables at lunchtime, and two teaspoonfuls of baby rice mixed with milk at teatime. This was too little and did not include any form of protein, which is essential for a baby aged seven months and weighing 7.5kg (17lb).

Although she was exhausted trying to deal with two sleepless children, David's mother followed my advice and made two batches of chicken and vegetable casserole and two batches of lentil and vegetable casserole. Within two days of introducing this food at lunchtime, David began to drink less milk in the night. She gradually increased his lunchtime solids to six tablespoonfuls of chicken or lentil casserole and his teatime baby rice was replaced with six teaspoonfuls of a proper carbohydrate tea. These amounts were much more realistic for a baby of David's age and weight. Although he continued to wake for a further four nights at 10pm, his mother was able to settle him back to sleep with a small drink of cooled boiled water. Within a further three nights, David was back to sleeping from 7pm to 7am.

I believe that the main cause of David's sudden night-time waking was genuine hunger caused by not receiving the correct amounts of the right sort of food for his age and weight. In my experience, the occasional *use of convenience food is fine, but babies who are being fed constantly from jars and packets are much more likely to develop sleep problems related to feeding.*

Hunger at nine to 12 months

Feed times: 7am, 11.45am/12pm, 2.30pm, 5pm, 6.30pm (plus any middle-of-the-night feeds necessary)

Nap times between 7am and 7pm: 9.30am–10am, 12.30pm–2.30pm
Maximum daily sleep: 2–2½ hours

(These times are only meant as a guide. Adjust the times to suit your baby's individual needs.)

Parents often assume that hunger is unlikely to be a cause of crying once their baby is successfully weaned, but this is not always the case. Your baby should be sleeping through the night by this age, and if he is waking and crying or is crying a lot during the day, do make sure you eliminate hunger as a cause before looking at other possibilities.

* If your baby is waking and crying at night, or is waking before 7am, then he may be hungry. If you are still breast-feeding, this could be due to low milk supply.

* Check that you are meeting your baby's nutritional needs, especially the protein and carbohydrate content of his diet. He needs daily protein and a high-carbohydrate teatime meal based on pasta, rice or potatoes to help fill him up so that he is not woken by hunger in the night.

* Home-cooked food has a higher density and is more sustaining than shop-bought food. I find that serving more home-cooked food to a baby who is largely fed shop-bought food will better satisfy his hunger.

* If your baby is not taking a big enough milk feed before bedtime, hunger can often cause early morning waking.

* Keep offering a variety of foods to ensure he doesn't get hungry, but remember that towards the end of his first year, your baby's growth rate will begin to slow down, and he will start to eat less as he moves on from puréed food.

Throughout the first year hunger is one of the most common causes of crying. I would always suggest considering hunger as a possibility if your baby is unsettled, and that you only work through the other issues that may cause distress once you are certain that your baby is not crying because he is hungry. Hunger is one of the easiest problems to solve, and a fretful, hungry baby will quickly become contented once his hunger is satisfied.

2
Sleep

Getting enough sleep is essential for your baby's mental and physical development, and an overtired baby soon becomes an unhappy baby. Sleep problems are very common in the first year, and parents often lack confidence in dealing with a baby who isn't sleeping well. Settling your baby into a routine helps you to become far more aware of his natural sleep rhythms and, as a result, you will know when he is crying due to lack of sleep or overtiredness.

The amount of sleep your baby needs changes throughout

the first year as he grows and develops. If your baby gets too tired, he won't be able to feed effectively, making it harder for him to sleep. A baby who sleeps well will quickly become happier and more contented.

Initially, you may not always be able to tell when your newborn baby is tired, but as he gets older, there are some common signs that you can look out for:

✿ He may start yawning.

✿ He may rub his eyes, or pull at his ears.

✿ He may become fretful.

✿ He may lose interest in what is going on around him.

✿ He may become quieter and seem to slow down.

✿ He may resist any attempts to soothe him.

You will probably find that you start to recognise your own baby's signs of tiredness fairly quickly, and be able to tell if he is ready to sleep. What can be more difficult is dealing with overtiredness, as this can make a baby inconsolable and very hard to settle.

Sleep in the first two months

Feed times: 7am, 10am/11am, 2pm/2.30pm, 5pm, 6pm/6.15pm, 10pm/11pm (plus any middle-of-the-night feeds necessary)

Nap times between 7am and 7pm: 8.30/9am–10am, 11.30am/12pm–2.30pm, 3.30/4.30pm–5pm
Maximum daily sleep: 3½–5½ hours

(These times are only meant as a guide. Adjust the times to suit your baby's individual needs.)

Most babies need around 16 hours sleep a day during the first few weeks, although this is an average and some may need more or less. Babies under six weeks will usually start to get tired after an hour of being awake and although they may not be quite ready to sleep, they should be kept quiet and calm once they have been awake for this long.

I do not believe that young babies should ever be left to cry for long periods of time in order to get themselves off to sleep. What I would recommend for an overtired baby is five or 10 minutes of 'crying down' time (provided I know he has been well-fed and winded), but no more than this. If he hasn't dozed off after a short period of 'crying down' time, you should pick him up and calm him for a few minutes, then try resettling him again.

Crying down

Dr Brian Symon, a senior lecturer at the University of Adelaide and author of Silent Nights, *an infant sleep* guide, uses the term 'crying down' to describe the pattern of crying when an overtired baby is going to sleep.

The overtired baby will start to bellow loudly when put down to sleep. He will cry loudly for a long spell then go quiet for a short spell. If he is ignored, the crying will start again but quieter. He will continue to do this, crying and then going quiet, but the crying will gradually decrease in volume, and the gaps between cries will become longer until he no longer cries at all.

The process of crying down to sleep takes between 10 and 30 minutes. The more overtired the baby is, the louder and longer he will cry. Parents who find the crying difficult to ignore are advised to wait 10 minutes before going in to him. They can then enter and reassure the baby with a soothing touch or quiet voice but only for a maximum of one to two minutes. Parents should then wait a further 10–15 minutes before returning. For this *technique to work it is essential that the baby is not picked up and that he is allowed to settle by himself in his bed.*

In my experience, crying down to sleep usually takes no longer than five to 10 minutes.

Tiredness in young babies

✿ Babies don't always show obvious signs of tiredness, but if your baby is crying and has been awake for more than an hour, I would advise trying to help him wind down gradually. Make sure there aren't too many distractions and that it is quiet and peaceful. This will help him get ready to sleep.

✿ Sometimes parents react to crying by stimulating their baby, and this can make things far worse if he is already feeling tired. Think about how much your baby has slept and whether tiredness could be causing the crying before you start trying to distract him with games or loud noises.

* Babies who are prone to catnapping during the day are more likely to get overtired, and this can lead to excessive crying during the early evening, which can often be mistaken for colic.

* Babies of under three months should not be allowed to stay awake for more than two hours at a time. If they are awake for longer than this, they often get overtired and start to fight sleep. An overtired baby can soon become inconsolable.

Too much daytime sleep

Even very young babies need to be awake for some time during the day. Too much daytime sleep may be the cause of your baby being wide awake, and crying, during the night.

* If a baby is allowed to sleep for very long spells between feeds in the daytime, it is more likely that he will wake up for long spells during the night. Try to encourage your

baby to stay awake for at least an hour after each
daytime feed.

* Try to limit daytime sleep to no more than five hours
between 7am and 7pm.

* By around four weeks, your baby will probably start to stay
awake for longer periods and will seem more alert. It is
important to encourage this wakefulness during the day in
order to ensure his night-time sleep is not affected.

Assisted sleep routine

*A baby who is not established on a sleep routine can
sometimes end up sleeping too long during the day and
therefore crying and not sleeping well in the early
evening. In my experience, the only way to reverse this
with a very young baby is to assist him to sleep in the*

evening, between 7pm and 10pm, for several nights.

Assisting your baby to sleep involves settling him in your arms and continuing to hold him as he sleeps for a good two or three hours. Make sure you are in a comfortable seat when you do this and do not pass him to another person as this will unsettle him. After a few nights of sleeping in your arms you can then settle him in his bed, but keep him next to you so you can quickly reassure him if he stirs.

While you are doing this in the evening, it is also important to reduce his daytime sleep slightly. Instead of a long nap between 8am and 10am, allow him a short nap of 20–30 minutes at 8am and a further nap of 15 minutes at around 10am. In the afternoon, instead of a long nap between 3pm and 5pm, allow him two naps of 20–30 minutes at around 3pm and 4.30pm. You may need to give him additional top-up feeds between these nap times to keep him happy. You should also offer him additional top-up feeds prior to nap times and after his bath to ensure he is not resisting sleep due to hunger.

If you are consistent with these methods, within a week you should find your baby is sleeping well between 7pm and 10pm, awake and feeding well between 10pm and 11pm, settles to sleep easily and sleeps a good stretch in the night before needing to feed again. In my experience, as a baby's night-time sleep improves, you should find it easier to keep him awake for longer during the day after feeds, allowing you to establish proper scheduled nap times for his age.

Early morning waking

Having a baby who wakes up crying excessively very early every morning is stressful for both mother and baby.

* In my experience, most babies tend to drift into light sleep between 5am and 6am and if they wake up and are fed as if this is the start of the day, they will become over-stimulated and won't go back to sleep. I recommend dealing with any waking before 7am as if it were night time, and feeding your baby quickly and quietly without talking to him.

* Sometimes hunger causes early morning waking and crying. In young babies, this can be the result of too small a feed in the middle of the night.

The right environment

* Even a chink of light getting into the room can mean your baby will wake at dawn as the sun rises, and this is why I always advocate the use of black-out blinds.

* Although some babies do manage to sleep in the bustle of a busy household, others will find it difficult. Try to ensure your baby has some peace and quiet when he is going to sleep or he may find it difficult to get a proper rest.

❖ Somewhere during your baby's second month, you may notice that he drifts into light sleep every 30–45 minutes. Most babies, if allowed, learn to settle themselves back to sleep provided they are not hungry. If you rush to your baby too soon and help him back to sleep by rocking or patting, or giving him a dummy, you can cause sleep association problems. In the long term, this may mean that your baby starts waking up not just for a feed but also every time he comes into a period of light sleep, and that you have to keep getting up in the night to help him go back to sleep.

Case study: Emily, aged six weeks
Problem: Early morning waking

Emily went straight into the two-to-four week Contented Little Baby *routine as she was a big baby at birth,*

weighing close to 4.5kg (10lb). She fed well and slept
well and was soon sleeping through till 6.30–7.30am
from the 10pm feed. However, she began waking earlier
and earlier each morning, until she was up at 5am and
would not go back to sleep until nearly 6.30am. She
would then sleep for an hour, and from 7.30am would
follow her routine. She was feeding well and gaining
weight, but when she was woken for her 10pm feed
she drank her milk very quickly. She soon became
sleepy, taking the last 30ml (1oz) in a very drowsy state
and was asleep again by 10.35pm.

I came to the conclusion that this quick and rather
sleepy feed was the cause of Emily's early morning
waking. Until a baby is between three and four months
old, she may need to wake up properly somewhere
between 7pm and 7am. I suggested to her parents that
for the following week they should wake Emily as normal

at 10pm but not feed her until 10.20pm. This would ensure that she was properly awake before she began feeding. They should give her two-thirds of the feed before her nappy change. Then, instead of giving her the remainder straight away, they should wait 15–20 minutes. After this, they should dim the lights and offer the remainder of her feed and settle her back in bed by 11.30pm. Within three nights Emily was back to sleeping right through to 7am.

I advised Emily's parents to continue with this longer waking at 10pm for a further couple of weeks and then gradually reduce the length of time she was awake by 10 minutes every three days. By the time she reached three months, Emily was able to sleep through to 7am with a 30-minute waking at the 10pm feed.

Sleep at three to four months

Feed times: 7am, 11am, 2.15/2.30pm, 6.15pm, 10/10.30pm (plus any middle-of-the-night feeds necessary)

Nap times between 7am and 7pm: 9am–9.45am, 12pm–2/2.15pm
Maximum daily sleep: 3 hours

(These times are only meant as a guide. Adjust the times to suit your baby's individual needs.)

In my experience, some parents start to have problems with their babies' sleep patterns when they reach eight to 12 weeks. At this stage of development, the baby's sleep pattern settles into an adult one with distinct stages of light and deep sleep.

* Your baby will come into a light sleep cycle at around 30–45 minutes. If he is not due for a feed or to be awake, try to allow him 10–15 minutes to resettle himself. Obviously, you can only do this if you are confident he is not waking due to hunger.

* Excessive night-time waking can become a problem at this age. If a baby has become dependent on his parents to help him get back to sleep at the end of his sleep cycle, he often starts waking up in the night when he drifts into light sleep because he can't settle himself without help. Learning the wrong sleep associations at this young age can quickly cause long-term sleep problems.

* By this age, most babies should be capable of sleeping nearer to 7am from their late feed, provided that their daytime sleep doesn't exceed three and a half hours, divided between two or three naps a day.

* A baby who is allowed to sleep too much in the day may become unsettled and wake up in the night. Likewise, a baby who sleeps too little may become overtired and unable to settle to sleep so well at night.

✿ By the time they reach 12 weeks, most babies only need a very short nap in the afternoon if they have slept well at lunchtime. The late afternoon nap is usually dropped when the baby is between three and six months of age.

Sleep at five to six months

Feed times: 7am, 11am, 2.15/2.30pm, 6.15pm, 10pm *(plus any middle-of-the-night feeds necessary)*

Nap times between 7am and 7pm: 9am–9.45am, 12pm–2/2.15pm
Maximum daily sleep: 2½–3 hours

(These times are only meant as a guide. Adjust the times to suit your baby's individual needs.)

The majority of babies of this age are capable of sleeping a long spell from their last feed to nearer 7am in the morning, provided they are feeding enough during the day and not having too much daytime sleep. If your baby is still waking up in the night, or has been sleeping through and suddenly starts waking up earlier, it is important to look at the amount of daytime sleep he is having. Some babies need as little as two and a half hours daytime sleep divided between two naps if they are to sleep well at night.

✿ Sometimes parents whose babies are awake and crying during the night at this age, assume that their baby must be hungry for solids and that starting to wean them early might solve the problem. However, it may also be that your baby's sleep patterns are not adjusted enough for his age or that he isn't taking sufficient milk.

✿ If your baby does not sleep well during the day, he can get overtired which means he will sleep very deeply as soon as he goes to bed. This can mean that he will wake up crying very early in the morning.

✿ If your baby is getting tired and fractious by 6.30pm in the evening, it is possible that he is not having enough daytime sleep.

✿ Teething can be a cause of crying at this age, and can lead to disruptive, sleepless nights. However, it shouldn't last for weeks on end. If what you had thought were teething problems seem to be lasting for longer, or are accompanied by other symptoms such as loss of appetite, diarrhoea or a fever, you should contact a doctor rather than just assuming these are teething-related issues.

Sleep training

If your baby is over six months and continues to wake up several times a night looking for a feed or has to be rocked back to sleep, it is possible that some sort of sleep training may be needed if long-term healthy sleep habits are to be established.

Sleep training, particularly if it involves eliminating night feeds, is not something that should be undertaken without great consideration, and certainly not until your baby is well established on three solids meals a day. It is important that you gradually reduce and eliminate night feeds so that your baby increases his daytime solids, before attempting any form of sleep training. Eliminating night feeds by controlled crying could result in your baby crying for hours through genuine hunger. Always use my assisted sleep routine method (see page 52) along with the core night method (see page 127) before attempting any form of sleep training. Other forms of sleep training, particularly controlled crying, should only be used as a last resort and after seeking advice from your GP or health visitor.

Sleep at seven to nine months

Feed times: 7am, 11.45am, 2.30pm, 5pm, 6.30pm, (10.30pm) (plus any middle-of-the-night feeds necessary)

Nap times between 7am and 7pm: 9.15/9.30am–9.45/10am, 12.30pm–2.30pm
Maximum daily sleep: 2½–2¾ hours

(These times are only meant as a guide. Adjust the times to suit your baby's individual needs.)

Disturbed sleep and night-time crying at this stage can often be caused by food-related problems. Indeed, many of the problems I come across in babies of seven to nine months are related to feeding and one of the main causes is not getting the balance right between milk and solids.

✿ If you introduce foods that are difficult to digest, such as bananas, avocado, tomatoes and protein-rich foods, earlier than recommended, this can lead to your baby waking up in the night and crying. In the early days of weaning, it is a good idea to keep a diary of what your baby eats so that you can spot any reactions to food swiftly.

✿ Cutting back too quickly on your baby's intake of milk during the day can also lead to night-time waking, as your baby will wake up needing milk during the night.

✿ If you feed your baby low-carbohydrate meals before bed, for example a vegetable soup served without extra potatoes or bread, he may not be able to sleep properly at night because he doesn't feel satisfied. I have found that there is a close link between food and sleep, and it is not just the quantities of food which are important, but making sure that the right balance of foods is given at the right times of day. For further information on establishing a healthy, balanced diet for your baby and feeding guides see *The Contented Little Baby Book of Weaning.*

* Feeding your baby large quantities of fruit and vegetables late in the day can cause him to wake up in the night or very early morning to poo.

* Too much commercially prepared food can lead to a low intake of protein, which again can lead to night-time waking.

* Sometimes babies of this age wake up at night crying because they are cold, having rolled around and thrown off their covers. That's why I recommend using a sleeping bag as your baby can move around unrestricted, but won't get chilly. Make sure you have the right tog of sleeping bag for the time of year.

* Too much daytime sleep can still cause a problem at this age. If your baby is sleeping in excess of three hours during the day, he may wake up crying at night because he is simply not tired.

* Try gradually reducing your baby's daytime sleep to see if this improves his sleeping at night. Sometimes babies of this age can need as little as two and a half hours of sleep during the day.

✿ Allowing your baby to sleep past 7am in the morning can also lead to him having too much daytime sleep. If he sleeps longer than this, you can gradually wake him up earlier until he gets used to it. He may be irritable for a short while, but in the long term if you cut back on the time he is asleep during the day, he will be less likely to wake up crying at night.

Sleep at nine to 12 months

Feed times: 7am, 11.45am/12pm, 2.30pm, 5pm, 6.30pm (plus any middle-of-the-night feeds necessary)

Nap times between 7am and 7pm: 9.30am–10am, 12.30pm–2.30pm
Maximum daily sleep: 2–2½ hours

(These times are only meant as a guide. Adjust the times to suit your baby's individual needs.)

The majority of babies cut back on the amount of daytime sleep they need at this age, and getting the right balance can often be difficult as two naps a day are often too much, yet they can not get through the day on only one nap. The first nap of the day is the one that should be reduced first, and you may find that if you continue with a longer morning nap that your baby starts to wake up early. A vicious circle quickly evolves where a baby actually needs the morning nap as he has woken early, but he wakes early because he is having too much daytime sleep.

* If your baby needs less sleep, cut back on the morning nap first. Sometimes babies start sleeping less at their lunchtime nap too, and they can get very tired and irritable during the late afternoon. If this happens, you may want to try cutting out the morning nap altogether so that your baby sleeps better at lunchtime.

* Babies are becoming more mobile by this stage of their development and sometimes, if they wake up in the night, they pull themselves up and then can't get back down again. This is quite a common cause of crying. You may need to help your baby settle himself down again for a while until he has learnt how to get himself back down again. Help him practise this by always putting him into the cot standing up. Then encourage him to grasp the bars

and, while supporting his hands, help him lower himself to a sitting position and roll over into a lying down position.

✿ I firmly believe that eating too many processed foods that contain high levels of sugar and additives can lead to poor night-time sleep. Too many sweets and chocolates, and large quantities of fruit juices or squashes, can also affect sleep patterns and lead to crying.

Case study: Morgan, aged 11 months
Problem: Early morning waking

Morgan had been a contented baby since birth and had always slept well until 7am. A month before his first birthday he dropped his morning nap and was sleeping well at lunchtime for around two hours. Soon after this, however, he began waking earlier in the morning and would not go back to sleep. He was waking at 5.30am ready to start the day, and would scream non-stop if left in his cot for more than 10 minutes. By lunchtime he was totally exhausted and would end up crying as he was being fed. Being awake from so early in the morning was having such a bad effect on the rest of his day that his mother had to reintroduce the morning nap. But this did not help the early morning waking; he continued to wake at 5.30am.

Morgan's mother contacted me in the hope that I could help. I explained that children of Morgan's age are extremely mobile and expending a great deal of energy at a time when their sleep requirements drop, making daytime sleep a difficult juggling act. I felt that Morgan was ready to drop his morning nap, but that he was not quite able to make it through the day without becoming overtired by bedtime, causing him to fall into a deep, exhausted sleep at 7pm. This caused him to wake early and it quickly became his habit to wake at 5.30am.

Following my advice, Morgan was put to bed at the earlier time of 6.40pm. On the first evening, he chattered until 7.05pm before falling asleep. The following morning he woke up at the earlier time of 5am as I thought he would, but after giving him a quick feed as I had advised, he returned to sleep at 6.10am, finally waking at 7.10am. I explained that putting Morgan to bed early was only a temporary measure, and once he was sleeping more between his usual waking time of 5.30am and 7am, his daytime sleep should be cut back immediately. I advised restricting his morning sleep to no more than 30 minutes should he wake at 5.30am and not settle back to sleep, and 15–20 minutes should he sleep nearer to 7am, or sleep on and off between 5am and 7am.

I explained that even if Morgan wasn't hungry, his mother should continue to offer milk to see if this would encourage him to return to sleep and provide a 'window of opportunity' for cutting back on his daytime sleep. On the second morning he woke at 5.30am and was given milk, he returned to sleep at 6.10am and slept until 7.00am when he was woken. He then took a 15-minute morning nap, slept for just under two hours at lunchtime and went to sleep at 6.45pm. The third morning he woke at 6.25am and was given a 10-minute morning nap and slept for two hours at lunchtime. That evening Morgan was put to bed at 6.45pm, he chatted until 7.10pm before going to sleep. He slept soundly until 6.30am the following morning. Morgan was put to bed at 6.45pm for a further week, and he would usually chatter for between 10–15 minutes before falling asleep.

He continued to sleep consistently until 6.15/6.20am, taking a 10–15-minute morning nap at 9.45am. While this pattern was emerging, I advised Morgan's parents to keep a detailed diary of Morgan's sleeping times to ensure that his bedtime was being extended closer to 7pm again. A week later he was being put in the cot at 7pm, and would fall asleep nearer to 7.15pm. The following morning he slept until 6.50am and, as I advised, was not given a morning nap, but his lunch and nap were brought forward to avoid him becoming overtired.

The process of encouraging Morgan to sleep later in the morning took three weeks of being persistent and consistent with his daytime naps, eliminating the morning nap when he slept soundly to nearer 7am, and allowing only 10 minutes if he woke earlier than that. By the third week he was waking nearer 7am most mornings, and managing to go down awake at 7pm in the evenings, falling asleep after 10–15 minutes of chattering. By the fourth week he was consistently sleeping until 7am every morning.

What else can affect your baby's sleep and lead to crying?

I've covered a number of the main issues that can disrupt your baby's sleep patterns at different stages of his development. There are some other issues that often cause sleep problems for babies during their first year.

✿ *Temperature.* If your baby is too hot or too cold, he will have problems sleeping or staying asleep. In hot weather, a nappy and T-shirt is usually enough clothing for your baby during the early part of the night. He may need a light-weight sleeping bag, thin blanket or sheet during the night.

✿ *Uncomfortable clothing.* Babies have sensitive skins, and if they have buttons on the back of their clothing, large collars or fancy ribbons, this can cause irritation and affect their sleep. The elastic waist of pyjama bottoms can be uncomfortable, too. You should also make sure that you remove labels from clothes as they can scratch.

* *Toys and activity centres.* If you have activity centres or toys in your baby's cot, you should remove them when he goes to sleep so that they don't distract him. The FSID (Foundation for the Study of Infant Deaths) recommends that you do not put pillows and toys in the cot.

* *Nappy rash.* This can be really painful if the skin becomes very red or is broken and can unsettle a baby. When this happens, clean your baby's bottom using baby oil instead of water. If you change your baby's nappy frequently and use a good barrier cream, the rash should heal up within a few days. If your baby has persistent problems with this, you should see your doctor.

* *Illness.* I believe that a sick baby needs more sleep, but when your baby is ill, he may find it hard to settle. Even simple coughs or colds can be very distressing for small babies, and may make it difficult for them to sleep through the night (see pages 147–9).

After hunger, tiredness is the most common problem that can lead to crying. As we have seen, your baby's sleep requirements and patterns change a lot during the first year, and it is important to be aware of this and to make sure your baby is getting all the sleep that he needs.

3
Stimulation

The first year of a baby's life is a time of very rapid development, and the amount of stimulation that he needs will increase as he grows and develops. In the first few weeks of life, most of his waking time will be taken up with feeding and nappy changing, and if he is overstimulated he may quickly become fractious and overtired. As your baby grows and is more aware of his surroundings, he will be fascinated by the world around him and will need more stimulation and interaction. It's important to get the balance right so your baby does not become overstimulated in the first year. A baby who is constantly overstimulated during the day, will often become very fretful and difficult to settle to sleep at night. You should keep a careful balance between social activity and quieter times during the day.

Parents are not always aware of how tired a small baby can get when those around him keep trying to interact with him. Babies, like adults, sometimes need some quiet time when they are awake and overstimulation during this time could cause them to become fretful and cry. Equally, an older baby may cry from sheer boredom if he is left lying awake and alone. How much interaction your baby needs will depend on his personality and his stage of development, and it is important to get the balance right to ensure that your baby remains happy and contented.

Stimulation in the first two months

Newborn babies don't need lots of toys or games as their waking hours tend to be focused on feeding. Just talking to your baby, singing to him or cuddling him, or even a simple cot book or mobile, will be sufficient to occupy and interest him. By the end of the second month, your baby's vision and hearing will have improved and he will be more interested in looking and listening; he may start smiling and will interact more with family and friends. It is very easy to give babies of this age too much in the way of stimulation, as they can easily get overtired if they don't have the rest and sleep that they need.

* Your baby can usually only stay awake for about an hour at a time at this age. If you think how much of that time will be occupied with feeding and changing nappies, you will see that there is not a great deal of time left and your newborn baby won't need much stimulation.

* Although your baby may sometimes be up and alert for more than an hour, try not to let him stay awake for more than two hours at a time as he is likely to end up exhausted and will find it hard to settle.

* All babies need cuddling and physical contact as it is a vital part of bonding, but make sure you are not keeping a tired baby awake with too much interaction.

* Of course friends and relatives will want to come and see your baby, but don't feel that you have to get him up for visitors. Try to arrange visitors during his awake time. It is really important that he gets all the sleep he needs. Sometimes when guests come to see a small baby, he is handed from person to person and cooed at and cuddled for a considerable time. Although he may not react immediately, you may find that he will start screaming soon afterwards as the stimulation has exhausted him. Once your baby is in this overtired and overstimulated state, it can be very hard to settle him to sleep.

* Don't let yourself get overloaded with visitors at this time. The most important thing is that he bonds with you and learns his cues for sleeping and feeding. If your routine is being constantly disrupted by well-meaning visitors, you may end up with a fretful baby.

* Newborn babies often receive piles of toys, but don't over-stimulate him by trying to show him everything all at once. It is better for him to get used to a few familiar toys.

* Be particularly careful not to overstimulate your baby close to bedtime by playing exciting games or making lots of loud noises. You should start winding down before bedtime, lowering the lights and closing the blinds or curtains so that it is easier for your baby to settle.

* Your baby will be most fascinated by you and will enjoy looking at your face. You should talk to him, smile and make eye contact, you may want to sing to him or show him a toy, but make sure you focus on playing with him at times when he is fully awake and lively and keep things very low-key prior to nap times and during night feeds.

* Even at such an early age, it is possible for a baby to get bored. Black-and-white soft picture books that are specially designed for this age range, brightly coloured musical mobiles, rattles or a play gym are good choices for very young babies.

Stimulation from three to four months

Your baby will become more able to express his needs during his third and fourth months. He will smile and gurgle and will be able to stay awake for longer. He will start to enjoy games and songs and as he gains control of his own body, his hand-to-eye co-ordination will develop. He will also start to anticipate what is happening during his day, and a routine can help with this in terms of establishing times of wakefulness and times for sleeping.

As your baby becomes more responsive, it is rewarding to interact with him as he will smile, laugh or make noises. Try to remember that he will still get tired very quickly. If you are aware of this you can make sure that your playtimes don't end up keeping him awake when he starts to need sleep, as this can lead to an unhappy, fractious baby.

It is equally important to make sure that your baby has plenty to occupy him when he is lively and awake as he will be fascinated by his surroundings at this time of rapid mental and physical development.

* Your baby will still need two or three naps during the day and will sleep for up to three hours in total. At this age he could, if allowed, stay awake for longer and even miss a nap, but he may be tearful and overtired later in the day and may find it hard to settle.

* Adults sometimes think that babies can sleep through anything, and although this may have been true in the first couple of months, you may find that noises wake your baby as he gets a little older. Try to let him nap in a quiet environment without the stimulus of lots of loud household noise as this will enable him to sleep more soundly.

* Be careful not to overstimulate your baby in the 20 minutes prior to naps. He will need time to wind down in order to settle easily. If he is overstimulated at this time, he is likely to find it difficult to get to sleep and this often results in crying.

* Try to find some quiet activities when your baby is getting ready to sleep or has been awake for a while. Singing a

gentle lullaby or reading him a short story may help him to relax. Make bathtime a calm affair without lots of games.

✿ Your baby is likely to be in his most wakeful phase about an hour after he has woken and been fed. This is the ideal time to get out some toys and books for up to 30 minutes, leaving you half an hour for winding down before his next nap.

✿ Babies have quite short concentration spans. If you are constantly handling your baby and talking to him during his waking time, he may soon become overstimulated. You need to watch him for signs of tiredness, and to take your cues from your baby.

Signs that your baby is overtired or overstimulated

- *Has been awake for more than two hours*
- *Excessive crying and can't be calmed down*
- *Unable to drift off to sleep naturally and seems to 'fight' sleep*

✿ At this stage, babies can start to get distracted by their surroundings making feeding more difficult. If he doesn't have enough milk because he's been distracted, you may need to offer him a top-up in a quiet room prior to his nap to avoid hunger later on.

✿ Babies do need stimulation during their wakeful periods, and at this age your baby will start to really enjoy games like 'peekaboo'. You can buy many toys and games aimed at this age group, but play gyms and small soft toys with different textures are the most popular. Your baby will start to be able to hold things himself, and may also enjoy toys that make noises.

Stimulation from five to six months

This is likely to be a busy time in your baby's development. He will gain more physical control of his body and may start sitting, aided at first. The other major change at six months is the introduction of solid foods (see page 35). Some working mothers will return to work after maternity leave at around this time. These major changes in your baby's life can be tiring, and it is important to be aware of this and to check that your baby doesn't get overstimulated.

* Your baby will need about two and half to three hours of sleep between 7am and 7pm, ideally in two separate naps. He is able to concentrate for longer and may be happy staying awake for more than two hours at a time now, but do watch for signs of tiredness if he's awake for a longer period, and make sure you don't overstimulate him.

* If your baby is starting nursery, or is going to be with a nanny or a childminder for the first time, he is likely to get more tired with this change to his regime, at least initially. It can be tempting to play with your baby as soon as you get home from work, as you may feel you have missed out on this during the day, but remember that your baby will probably need some peaceful time with you after all the stimulation of new and different daytime surroundings.

* Babies of this age still need up to 20 minutes to wind down before they are ready for bed. If they are overstimulated during this time, they will find it hard to settle.

* Your baby is growing more aware of what is going on around him, and may start to get bored if he feels he is being left out of things. Try alternating his position and moving him from room to room with you every 10 minutes to keep him stimulated.

* At five to six months, a baby can be quite demanding of your attention as he isn't able to do everything he would like to be able to himself and is starting to understand this. Babies can get very frustrated as they are more active, but still can't manage to move themselves around. If you can keep your baby occupied, this will minimise his feelings of frustration.

* Make sure you keep your baby stimulated during his wakeful times. He will really enjoy action games and songs, looking at books and pictures and will now start to be ready for other toys, such as cubes or bricks.

Stimulation from seven to nine months

During this phase of their development, babies can start to get bored very easily, and keeping them happily and safely occupied can be more of a problem than overstimulation. Your baby will gain more physical control of his body, and may start crawling or trying to move around. He may need more attention because he can get frustrated if he can't reach things he wants. His personality will start to become more apparent, and he will enjoy company.

✿ Babies still need two and a half to three hours of day-time sleep between 7am and 7pm at this age. This is best taken in two naps, ideally with a longer one after lunch. If they aren't getting enough sleep or are being overstimulated, babies can quickly become unhappy and fretful.

✿ The bedtime routine is still a vital part of the day if your baby is to settle down easily.

* Your baby should be able to amuse himself for short periods of time now, but don't expect him to be able to play alone for long as he will probably get bored fairly quickly.

* Babies become more interested in one another at this stage, and it is important to introduce your baby to other children. Babies enjoy spending time together but their interest can lead them to grab or poke one another, so you do need to keep an eye out to make sure that they don't inadvertently hurt one another.

* Babies of this age are rapidly gaining dexterity and it is important to encourage this. Your baby may enjoy stacking bricks or pushing around cars.

* Your baby may start to crawl or 'bottom shuffle' and he may roll over to get toys that are out of his reach. He may also try to pull himself up on furniture. Babies some-times get distressed and angry if they can't move about in the way they'd like to, and frustration can often lead to crying.

- At mealtimes, your baby may want to feed himself and you should be giving lots of finger foods. This can be very messy, but do encourage your baby as it is part of his development and will help keep him stimulated.

- Flap books or soft activity books with things to feel or Velcro fastenings to undo are often popular with this age group, and will occupy your baby.

- It is important to be aware that your baby likes to be active and engaged. If you are busy cooking in the kitchen, you can keep him happy with plastic pots, bowls and beakers, boxes and wooden spoons.

- If you are struggling to keep your baby occupied, you will find a wide variety of classes, such as baby gym, singing or music groups. These will help to ensure that your baby doesn't get bored, although you may discover that he finds the other babies just as fascinating as the class itself!

Stimulation from 10 to 12 months

As your baby approaches the end of his first year, he is moving towards becoming a toddler and will enjoy demonstrating his independence. He will be able to communicate with you more now. He will have learnt how to get your attention if he wants something, and will certainly let you know when he isn't happy. He will be far more mobile and this can mean that he gets tired quite easily, so you should watch for this. However, it is equally true that your baby needs lots of stimulation at this age, as he can get bored very quickly.

✿ Babies of this age usually need two or three hours of sleep during the daytime, between 7am and 7pm or 8am and 8pm. This is usually best taken in two naps, with a shorter one in the morning and a longer one after lunch. However, if your baby starts to wake up in the night or early morning the amount of daytime sleep should be reduced. As he approaches the end of his first year, your baby may be ready to drop his morning nap or to just take a brief catnap in the morning. When this happens, you may find that he needs a longer nap after lunch for a while so that he doesn't get too tired.

* If for some reason a baby is only taking a short lunchtime nap of less than an hour than he may need another short nap of no more than 15 minutes in the late afternoon if overtiredness is to be avoided at bedtime.

* It is still important to continue your baby's normal bathtime and bedtime routine, and to make sure he has some time to wind down before he goes to sleep.

* Your baby is using more physical energy to move about now, which can be exhausting. Don't overstimulate him if he is starting to look tired – he will need some quiet time.

* Your baby will be able to occupy himself for longer now, and will start to be ready for toys like building blocks and balls. He will also enjoy action games and songs.

* It is important that you talk to your baby throughout the day about what you are doing as you do it. He will begin

to pick up on words and the more you talk to him, the more he will understand.

✿ Babies of this age can get extremely cross and often end up crying if they are prevented from doing what they want to do. You need to learn the art of distraction, of diverting your baby's attention towards something else. Having a favourite toy to hand, or just pointing at something that he may find interesting, will often be enough to distract him.

✿ If your baby seems to be having a lot of tearful outbursts, he may be getting bored. Have a think about his daytime routine. Could he be spending too much time indoors, or doing the same activities? I find that taking babies out for a short walk both in the morning and afternoon is great for dispelling boredom.

✿ Try to rotate your baby's toys to make sure he doesn't get bored by being given the same thing to play with every day. Although babies sometimes have a favourite toy that they want to play with over and over again, they still need the diversion of other toys or activities. This doesn't mean that you have to spend a small fortune on toys. You can encourage his natural curiosity with household objects such as empty plastic containers, egg boxes or cardboard tubes; babies often find these as much fun as expensive toys.

In my experience, babies need very different levels of stimulation as they progress through their first year, and that both overstimulation and boredom can cause crying. It may seem difficult to get the balance right, but you will soon learn to be guided by your baby and to spot the signs that tell you whether he needs more or less stimulation.

4
Feeding Problems:
wind, colic and reflux

There are some specific problems related to feeding that can lead to your baby crying, but it is important to have ruled out all the basic causes first, such as hunger (see Chapter 1) or tiredness (see Chapter 2). If you are faced with prolonged and inconsolable crying and are sure that your baby is not being affected by any of the factors I have already discussed, then it is time to look at some other possible causes of crying.

Wind is the most common problem relating to feeding as it can make your baby feel very uncomfortable and lead to crying. Many babies will suffer with wind at some stage, but it is not usually serious and can be eased by learning a good burping technique.

Excessive crying, or colic, is another common problem, particularly for babies who are under three months of age. Babies with colic can sometimes scream for hours on end, usually in the evening. There are a number of different theories about what causes colic, but I believe that settling your baby into a good routine will mean that he is far less likely to have problems with colic.

Reflux is often mistaken for colic, as some of the signs can be the same. Reflux is a kind of heartburn, and is only usually a problem in the first year. It can be very painful for your baby, and you may need medical advice to deal with it.

Wind

When a baby has air trapped in his tummy he will get wind. It is usually the result of him having gulped down too much air when feeding or, sometimes, when crying. It doesn't cause any harm to your baby, but it can be painful and make him really distressed. Most babies bring up their wind easily, but if your baby is troubled by wind and screams after a feed, try keeping him in a more upright position during the feed and while burping him.

Breast-fed babies

If you are breast-feeding your baby, he is less likely than a bottle-fed baby to suffer with wind, but certain issues can increase the possibility and being aware of these can help to prevent wind.

* A breast-fed baby does not take in as much air as a bottle-fed baby, and he may not need to bring up wind after every feed. If you have been trying to burp your baby for a few minutes and he seems perfectly happy, he may not need to bring up wind. If you keep interrupting your baby's feeds to try to get his wind up, he can end up so upset and frustrated that this will cause crying, and increase the chances of wind as he gulps down air.

* A breast-fed baby needs at least three hours to digest a full feed (this time is calculated from the beginning of one feed to the beginning of the next feed), so make sure you are not overfeeding him as this can cause wind. A sign that you are overfeeding your baby would be an excessive weight gain of 240–300g (8–10oz), week after week.

* Babies who are not positioned correctly to feed are more likely to be troubled by wind, so check that your baby is properly positioned and latched on.

* It is possible that your baby's wind can be caused by your diet, as certain foods can affect some babies. I have found that lots of citrus fruits or drinks, chocolate, dairy products or tomatoes in a mother's diet can lead to wind in some babies. Keep a food diary to try to identify if a particular food or drink is causing problems.

* You need to ensure you are eating a varied diet, without too many convenience foods, and consuming three healthy, balanced meals a day with snacks between meals.

* If your baby is drinking too much fore milk (see page 16) this can cause wind, so make sure he is feeding for long enough from the first breast and getting to the hind milk before switching to the second breast. It can take up to 25 minutes to get to the hind milk.

* A breast-fed baby will usually pull away from the breast when he is ready to burp. If he hasn't done this by the time he finishes feeding from the first breast, burp him before offering the second.

Bottle-fed babies

Babies who are fed formula milk are more likely to have problems with wind than those who are breast-fed. Sometimes simply changing bottles or teats, or altering the way you are feeding your baby, can help to alleviate wind.

* Bottle-fed babies tend to take in more wind than breast-fed babies, but there is no need for this to cause problems if they are given the opportunity to burp once during their feed and then again at the end.

- Make sure your baby is having the right amount of formula for his age and weight. Follow the instructions to make up the feed and shake the bottle well.

- If wind is a problem, try a wide-necked bottle with a specially designed teat to reduce the amount of air that the baby swallows.

- Before you feed your baby, undo the ring and teat and then screw them back on again to release any excess air.

- Make sure that you keep the bottle tilted when you feed your baby, ensuring that the teat is always full of milk.

- Try to keep your baby in a more upright position during and after feeding.

- A teat with a hole that is too large or too small for your baby could be a cause of excessive wind. You may find it helpful to try out some teats with different-sized holes.

- If you are already using an anti-colic bottle, the most common cause of wind is overfeeding. A formula-fed baby taking the recommended feed for his age and weight should manage to go between three and a half to four hours between feeds. Overfeeding could be causing a problem if your baby is gaining more than 240–300g (8–10oz) a week and he appears to be suffering from wind pains.

Tips for releasing trapped wind

Burping your baby is the best way to release trapped wind, but sometimes you may need to try a variety of methods:

* Sit your baby on your knee, with your hand across his chest and under his chin to support his head. Keeping his back straight, use your other hand to stroke his back firmly in an upward direction.

* Lie your baby flat on his back, and then slowly raise him up to a sitting position.

* Lie your baby on his tummy with his head to one side and gently rub his back.

✿ Colic drops may help to release trapped wind, but don't use these without discussing it with your health visitor first.

Colic

Excessive crying in babies who are under three months of age is often described as colic. A baby with colic may appear to be in considerable pain and will scream whilst bringing his knees up to his tummy. His tummy may be distended. The crying spells usually start during the late afternoon or early evening and can last for hours. It can be very distressing for parents as their babies are inconsolable, and it seems there is little that they can do to help.

There are many different views about what causes colic, and some healthcare experts do not even believe it exists at all. Some suggest it could be a physical problem caused by an immature digestive system, and say that the crying is probably due to intestinal pain. Some believe it could be a psychological issue, and that the baby is picking up on his parents' tensions. Others say colic is a perfectly natural phase of development without any cause or treatment, and that it is simply a matter of waiting for this stage to pass. You may hear a variety of thoughts on this, and many different solutions.

Signs of colic

If you think your baby has colic, you will know about it as the signs are usually quite clear.

* Your baby will cry excessively for long periods.

* The crying usually occurs during the late afternoon and evening, most often between about 6pm and midnight.

* Babies often thrash about and may bring their legs up in pain as if they have tummy ache.

* Your baby may have a noisy or distended tummy or pass lots of wind.

* Colic usually starts when babies are just two or three weeks old, and will gradually ease towards the end of the second month.

What can you do to help?

There is a lot of debate about how to help a baby who has colic, and you will probably hear all kinds of odd suggestions. Most experts agree that there is no magic cure for colic, and many say it is just something parents have to learn to live with as it will stop eventually. However, it can be very difficult for parents struggling with a screaming baby; sometimes it makes what ought to be one of the happiest times of their lives turn out to be one of the most miserable.

Parents often try feeding their baby, rocking or cuddling him, or taking him out for a walk in order to try to calm him and stop the crying. The problem with doing this is it rarely soothes the baby and can lead to the wrong sleep associations. Once the colic has disappeared, your baby may still expect to be fed, rocked or cuddled to sleep and this can continue for months, or even years.

People often ask me how I dealt with colicky babies and the honest answer is that not one of the many hundreds of babies I have helped care for has ever suffered from colic because I always resolved excessive crying by structuring their feeding and sleeping.

I believe there are a number of common causes of colic, and when parents ask me how to deal with their colicky baby, I have to tell them that the best thing they can do is to settle their baby into a routine. Most of them find that their baby's colic disappears immediately.

If you are experiencing problems with a colicky baby, I think there may be a number of reasons for this. If you eliminate all these possible causes, and follow the routine appropriate for your baby's age in *The New Contented Little Baby Book*, I think you will be able to alleviate the problem.

✿ Some breast-fed babies are unsettled during the evening because their mother's milk supply is low at this time. If you try topping up your baby with a bottle of expressed milk after his evening feed, you may find that things improve. If this is the case, you will know that low milk supply has been a problem and you should try to increase your supply by expressing.

* I believe colic is sometimes caused by a baby being given a feed before the previous one is digested – make sure you are leaving sufficient time between feeds so your baby can digest. If your baby is getting fretful an hour and a half after his feed it is very possible that this is due to tiredness and not hunger.

* Once your milk is in, it is important to ensure your baby empties the first breast before transferring him to the other breast so that he gets to the filling hind milk, not just the fore milk as this would leave him feeling hungry again far too soon. I believe this is a common cause of colic.

* I suggest that young babies should be given up to 25 minutes on the first breast before being transferred to the second breast for up to 15 minutes as this will ensure they get the right balance of fore milk and hind milk.

* Your baby's afternoon feed should be given no later than 2.15pm as this will ensure that he will have a really good feed in the early evening.

* If your baby sleeps late in the morning, by 7pm he may have slept too much and not be ready to settle. If you wake him up at 7am even if he hasn't slept well in the night this will help ensure that he doesn't sleep too much during the day and is therefore ready to settle at 7pm.

* Overstimulation just before bedtime can result in an over-tired baby. Make sure you start to wind things down at this time of day. Until your baby is settled into a routine, it is better if one person does the bath, feeding and settling as constant handing from one person to another will only make a fretful baby worse.

* Babies who are overtired will find it hard to settle in the evening, and those who catnap on and off throughout the day are more likely to become overtired. Settling your baby into a routine will help to solve this.

* If your baby screams every time you feed him and arches his back, he may be suffering with reflux (see page 119). You should get medical advice if you think this may be the case.

Case study: Beatrice, aged four weeks
Problem: Suspected colic

Beatrice, who weighed 2.7kg (6lb) at birth, was put onto a strict four-hourly feeding routine (not a CLB routine) within a week of being born. For the first three weeks, she fed and slept well, waking only once in the night after her 10pm feed. Between the third and fourth week, Beatrice started to become more unsettled, sometimes screaming long before feeds were due. Then when offered a feed, she would only drink around 120ml (4oz) of her usual 180ml (6oz) feed before becoming very upset. She would scream and bring her legs up to her chest as if in pain. It could take Christina, her mother, up to an hour to get Beatrice to take a 120ml (4oz) feed.

Christina contacted me when Beatrice was four weeks old, and she was becoming more and more

Leabharlanna Fhine Gall

*difficult to feed and settle for naps and in the evening.
Beatrice, who had previously always settled well at
6.30pm, would often cry on and off for two hours before
she eventually fell asleep. Beatrice was being fed
150ml (5oz) at around 2/3am, then at 6am, 10am and
2pm. At 6pm Christina had increased her feed to 210ml
(7oz), in the belief that the reason Beatrice was not
settling at 6.30pm was because she was hungry. She
would then take a dream feed of 120ml (4oz) at 10pm.
Her daily total intake of milk was around 900ml (30oz)
a day.*

*Her mother, who had read that colic usually started
at around three weeks, was convinced that this was the
problem and contacted me when Beatrice was five
weeks old to see if I could offer any advice. The first
thing that I noticed was that Beatrice, who now weighed
4.3kg (9lb 8oz), had put on well over 1.5kg (3lb) in*

weight since birth. Her feeding and sleeping routine
looked like this:

2/3am	150ml (5oz)
5.45am	awake
6am	150ml (5oz)
7am	asleep
9am	awake
10am	150ml (5oz)
10.30am	asleep
1pm	awake
2pm	150ml (5oz)
2.30pm	asleep
4pm	awake
6pm	180ml (6oz) over a period of two hours
9pm	would fall asleep exhausted after two to three hours of intermittent crying
10pm	120ml (4oz) – dream feed

Although all babies are individuals and their feeding needs can vary, the guidelines of 75ml (2½oz) of formula milk per pound of the baby's body weight over a 24-hour period meant that Beatrice should have been taking a total of approximately 720ml (24oz) per day. The fact that Beatrice was taking 180ml (6oz) more each day, along with her weight gain of more than 10oz (280g) each week, and her tummy was very hard and distended at times, led me to believe that overfeeding was the main cause of the excessive crying periods.

The problem was also exacerbated by the times of the feeds. For the first three weeks when Beatrice was fed at 6am, she was put back to bed to sleep until the next feed at 10am. By the time she reached three weeks, she was starting to cut back on her daytime sleep and had started waking up earlier and earlier, until she was regularly waking up at 9am. Christina, who was determined to keep her in a strict four-hourly feeding pattern, would not feed her until 10am. This caused two problems – a baby as young as five weeks, even if not quite ready for a feed, will automatically look for a feed when she wakes, and secondly, babies of this age usually start to get tired after being awake for an hour and a half. I believe that Beatrice, who had been awake from 9am, would be getting tired halfway through her feed and would want to go to sleep the minute she started to feel full. This usually occurred once she had taken 120ml (4oz), which is much nearer the recommended amount for her weight than the 150ml (5oz) that her mother was making her take.

The rest of the nap times, along with the large feeds, had a knock-on effect on Beatrice, which led to her not settling at bedtime and crying excessively. Because Beatrice was awake from 4pm in the afternoon, trying to feed her two hours after she had woken up meant that she was very overtired for the 6pm feed. I believe that this, along with constantly offering more milk at that time, caused much of the distress and any possible pain she may have been experiencing.

I suggested that Christina alter the sleeping times during the day and, apart from the bedtime feed and late feed, she should try to offer no more than 120ml (4oz) a feed, aiming for a daily total of between 720ml (24oz) to 800ml (27oz) of milk. At no time should Beatrice be made to feed more than she needs. If for some reason she took a lot less than the recommended amounts, she could be topped up with a small amount prior to her morning or lunchtime nap. Overleaf is an example of the suggested times and amounts for sleeping and feeding.

2/3am	120ml (4oz)
6am	120ml (4oz) – only as much as the baby needs to settle back to sleep
6.30am	settle back to sleep
7.30am	30–60ml (1–2oz) top-up before 8am (not to be forced)
9am	sleep
10.30am	120ml (4oz)
11.30am	sleep
2pm	120ml (4oz)
3.30/4pm	sleep
5pm	90ml (3oz) – only as much as baby needs to keep her calm for bath at 5.45pm
6.15pm	50ml (1½oz) top-up feed
6.30pm	settle in cot no later than 6.45pm
10pm	120ml (4oz)

During the first week of following the new feeding and sleeping times, Beatrice continued to wake up at between 2 and 3am, and then at 6am, and take a 120ml (4oz) feed at both of these times. Sometimes she would not take a top-up at 7.30/8am and Christina would have to feed her early at 10am, and then top her up just prior to the lunchtime nap; otherwise she found that Beatrice would only sleep for an hour and a half at lunchtime.

Christina saw an almost instant change to Beatrice's feeding and sleeping during the day, with little or no crying, but it did take a further week to get the settling at bedtime sorted out. Although Beatrice did not cry with the same intensity, and Christina was convinced that she was not in pain as she used to be, it was still taking over an hour for her to fall asleep. I suggested that Christina should try to push her afternoon nap closer to

4pm, so that it was reduced by 30 minutes, and allow no more than one hour. She should also ensure that Beatrice was in her bed no later than 6.45pm.

By the time Beatrice was seven weeks old, she was settling well in the evening and at all nap times. I advised Christina that when Beatrice went through a growth spurt, she should first increase the 6/7am feed by 30ml (1oz), then once Beatrice was regularly drinking the new increased amount, she should increase the 10/11am feed by 30ml (1oz). The third feed to increase would be the split feed at bedtime. By increasing the feeds in this order, it would ensure that Beatrice did not need to feed more in the middle of the night when she went through a growth spurt. I also said that a small top-up feed before the lunchtime nap was fine if Beatrice would not take a full feed, as it would help keep her sleep on track.

It is very easy to overfeed a formula-fed baby. Although some babies may need to drink slightly more than the recommended amounts, if a baby is drinking an awful lot more than suggested for his age it could well be the cause of excessive crying and possibly some physical discomfort, too.

If your baby is gaining an excessive amount of weight each week and suffers from painful wind, it is possible that overfeeding is the problem, particularly if he is feeding more than two or three times after midnight. Eliminating feeds using the 'core night' method (see page 127) can help to resolve the problem of excessive night-time feeding.

Reflux

Sometimes a baby displaying all the symptoms of colic actually has a condition called gastro-oesophageal reflux. This can affect both breast- and bottle-fed babies and is very much like heartburn. Because the valve at the lower end of the oesophagus is too weak to keep the milk in the baby's stomach, it comes back up, along with the acid from the stomach, causing a very painful burning sensation in the oesophagus. It occurs because this valve isn't fully developed, and reflux will usually ease as your baby grows and the valve gets stronger.

Symptoms

The symptoms of reflux can be similar to colic, as babies with reflux can seem unsettled and cry a lot. There are a number of other more specific signs that you can look out for:

* Excessive possetting or vomiting is a common symptom of reflux. However, not all babies with reflux will actually sick up the milk. This is known as 'silent reflux' and these babies can often be misdiagnosed as having colic.

* Babies with reflux can be difficult to feed. They may refuse to feed altogether, or will keep breaking off during feeding, arching their backs and screaming.

* They may have recurrent hiccups or cough a lot.

* They may have disturbed sleep.

✿ They often get irritable when laid flat, and no amount of cuddling or rocking will calm them when they are like this.

What can you do?

There are some steps that you can take to make sure that you are not doing anything to exacerbate your baby's reflux problem. Generally, reflux problems will gradually disappear by the end of the first year, although a few babies may still experience it up to the age of 12–18 months.

✿ Be careful not to overfeed your baby – you may need to offer smaller, more frequent feeds, which makes it easier for his body to cope.

✿ Make sure you wind him after feeding, and try to keep him sitting upright for 20 minutes after a feed.

✿ Avoid bouncing your baby about too much.

✿ Try using a specially designed sleep positioner for reflux babies in his bed to help with symptoms when he sleeps.

* If your baby has the symptoms of reflux, ask your doctor for a reflux test. I have seen too many cases of babies being diagnosed as having colic, when in fact they were suffering from reflux, despite not being sick.

* In the first instance, reflux is usually treated with feed thickeners. However, if the reflux is very severe, medication is normally prescribed. Make sure you see a paediatric doctor who specialises in reflux as your baby's dosage will need to be monitored and changed as he grows.

* Caring for a baby with reflux can be stressful but please be reassured that the majority of babies will outgrow it before the end of their first year.

Case study: Alice, aged six weeks
Problem: Silent reflux

Alice was four weeks old when I went to help care for her. I had helped look after her elder brother Patrick, then aged two, for six weeks when he was born. He had been a model baby and had gone into the routine from day one. He slept through the night at six weeks and had continued to do so ever since; he had always been a good feeder and a very easy baby. I felt confident that their mother would only need me for four weeks with the second baby, as she has always shown an excellent understanding of sleep rhythms, the importance of the right sleep associations and the correct structuring of feeds.

It therefore came as a bit of a shock when I arrived to find that Alice was not quite in 'the routine'. Her sleeping pattern was fine; she settled well at 7pm, I woke her at 10pm, she then fed well and would sleep until 5am then feed and settle quietly until 7am. Her lunchtime nap was also good. The problem was she would not be put down during the day. Her mother would have to carry her the whole time. After several days of helping care for Alice, I could see why she had to be held the whole time as the minute she was put down on the floor or in her bouncy chair, she would scream hysterically. Her mother was becoming increasingly worried about how she was going to cope in the long term with a very active toddler and a baby who refused to be put down for even a minute.

I suggested to her mother that it was possible that Alice was suffering from silent reflux, as she was showing some of the signs of reflux, and that she should have Alice checked over by her GP. The doctor totally dismissed the possibility of reflux as Alice was not bringing up any milk after feeds, and was sleeping well at night. He was of the opinion that Alice's behaviour was typical of many babies her age, and that in time she would calm down and the excessive crying would stop.

A week later, Alice's behaviour was getting even worse and I advised her mother that she should phone the surgery and demand a referral to a paediatrician. After a consultation with him, like the doctor, he was also adamant that Alice did not have reflux and suggested that we were spoiling her and that we should be stricter about leaving her in her chair. Over the two weeks that followed, despite very small feeds at 7pm and 10pm, Alice would continue to sleep well at night. However, the days got worse and she screamed and screamed and screamed. Things came to a head when she started to scream and arch her back the minute we tried to feed her. We went to see the paediatrician for the second time, as I was convinced that she did have silent reflux. He was still adamant and said it could *not be reflux because she was never sick. A further two weeks went past with Alice's behaviour getting worse and worse, and either her mother or I had to hold her virtually the whole of her waking time.*

A third visit was booked to the paediatrician. This time Alice's father accompanied us, and was insistent that a test be done to rule out reflux. The result came back positive; Alice had very serious reflux. She was prescribed medication and within a very short time, the intense crying had stopped, and she would happily spend short spells on her play mat looking at her toys. Her feeding also got easier.

The sad thing about Alice is that as a very small baby, she must have suffered a lot of pain. All too often babies are dismissed as being difficult or having colic, when in fact they are suffering from reflux. If your baby shows signs of behaviour similar to Alice, even if he is not bringing up milk, please do be insistent that you get a referral to a paediatrician. Reflux causes a huge amount of distress to young babies, and if your baby is crying a lot and showing some or all of the signs of reflux, it is important that the possibility is ruled out.

The 'core night' method

The core night method has been used for many years by maternity nurses and parents who believe in routine. It works on the principle that once a baby sleeps for one longer spell in the night, he should never again be fed during the hours slept in the course of the core night. If he wakes during those hours, he should be left for a few minutes to settle himself back to sleep. If he refuses to settle, then other methods apart from feeding should be used to settle him. Hollyer and Smith, authors of *Sleep: The Secret of Problem-free Nights*, in which the 'core night' is described, recommend patting, offering a dummy or giving a sip of cooled boiled water. Attention should be kept to the minimum while reassuring the baby that you are there. They claim that following this approach will, within days, have your baby sleeping at least the hours of his first core night. It also teaches the baby the most important of two sleep skills: how to go to sleep, and how to go back to sleep after surfacing from a non-REM (rapid eye movement) sleep.

Dr Brian Symon, author of *Silent Nights* and a senior lecturer in general practice at the University of Adelaide, recommends a similar approach for babies over six weeks. Babies who are putting on a good amount of weight each week, but who are still waking before 3am should be offered a dummy or some cooled boiled water. If the baby refuses to settle, he should then be given the shortest feed possible that will allow him to settle.

Neither of these methods of dealing with night feeding are new in babycare. Babycare expert Christine Bruell, who has advised over 35,000 mothers during her 40-year career, also advises offering cooled boiled water to a thriving baby over four weeks of age if he keeps regularly waking at 2am.

Before embarking on these methods, the following points should be read carefully to make sure that your baby really is capable of going for a longer spell in the night:

* These methods should never be used with a baby under one month or a baby who is not gaining weight. A baby not gaining weight should always be seen by a doctor.

* The above methods should only be used if your baby is regularly gaining 180–240g (6–8oz) each week, and if you are sure that his last feed is substantial enough to help him sleep for the longer stretch in the night.

* The main sign that a baby is ready to cut down on a night feed is a regular weight gain and the reluctance to feed, or feeding less at 7am.

* The aim of using any of the above methods is gradually to increase the length of time your baby can go from his last feed and not to eliminate the night feed in one go.

* The core night method can be used over three or four nights once your baby has slept a longer stretch from his

last feed for several nights in a row, and suddenly starts to wake up early again.

* If a baby is waking up several times in the middle of the night to feed, and losing interest in daytime feeds, it can be used to encourage longer spells between middle-of-the-night feeds.

* The core night method should only be used with a baby over one month who settles back to sleep quickly after taking a small amount of water. It should never be used with breast-fed babies who are not gaining over 180g (6oz) of weight each week or during growth spurts, as it could affect the amount of breastmilk a mother is producing.

* Babies under six months should not be allowed to consume large amounts of water as it could lead to a condition called water intoxication.

5
Separation Anxiety

At around the age of six months babies begin to become more understanding of their environment and realise that they are separate from their mothers. Between the ages of six and 12 months most babies show some signs of separation anxiety or stranger anxiety. You may find that your happy contented baby who was so easy-going and relaxed, and who would go to anyone, suddenly becomes clingy, anxious and demanding. He may start crying the minute you leave the room, or if he is approached by a stranger.

This sudden change in your baby's temperament can be very upsetting, but do be reassured that this behaviour is a totally normal part of a baby's development. All babies will go through this stage to some degree.

Although this can be a very exhausting time for you, it rarely lasts long. The following guidelines can help to make this difficult period less stressful.

✽ A comforter can be very reassuring to babies and provide a consistent comforting familiarity. By the time they reach one year, often a baby will choose one of his soft toys as a comforter. Consider introducing one if your child hasn't already made an attachment. Choose a toy that can be replaced (a spare cuddly toy that is interchanged regularly is a very sensible precaution) and that is washable and durable. Think of the practicalities. Safety is paramount – make sure that the comforter has no loose pieces that could be a choking hazard. It can be distressing for both your baby and for you if the comforter is mislaid so it might be worth encouraging your baby to leave it at home on trips to the park or on play dates.

✿ If you are planning to return to work when your baby is between six months and one year, try to make sure that he gets accustomed to being left with someone else before he reaches six months. If you are the sole carer, and he is not used to any other person looking after him for the majority of his day, it is more likely that he will find a prolonged separation upsetting. Think about arrangements that can work for you. If you are able to afford a little childcare it would be good to organise your weekly routine so that he spends some time with a nanny or childminder. Even if it is only a couple of hours a week. Alternatively, arrange with a friend a time when you look after each other's children. It is really helpful for your baby to begin to understand that you can leave and return. This minimises any anxiety not just for you but also for your baby, and it is good for him to interact with other babies.

* Aim to get your baby used to the nursery or childminder at least two weeks, and ideally a month, before returning to work. Gradually lengthen the period of time you leave him. If your childminder is able to support you with this, it will make the more prolonged absences easier for you both.

* The longer you give yourself and your child the time to get used to separation, the more flexibility it will give you. For instance if your baby is inconsolable by your departure you could delay trying to leave him again for a week or so. With such a young child, confidence and understanding is growing all the time, and it might be that if you leave it for a week or so, your baby has a different response next time.

* If your baby has a particular activity he enjoys – hitting a saucepan with a spoon, playing with a particular toy – try to organise for your baby's childminder or carer to have something similar to offer.

* Try role-playing. Even very young babies can grasp the concept of people or toys leaving and returning. Maybe

encourage your baby to say 'goodbye' to a doll or teddy, and then 'hello'.

* Praise your baby when he is prepared to go with your friend or the childminder.

* Talk to your baby. It is extraordinary how much a little baby can take in. If your baby is used to his father leaving for work each day, keep repeating 'Daddy has gone to work' and when he returns at the end of the day keep repeating 'Daddy is back from work'. This will reinforce his confidence that when the time comes for Mummy to go to work, you will always return.

* Role play can also play an important part. Saying 'hello' and 'goodbye' to your baby's favourite toys can also reinforce the fact that saying goodbye doesn't mean forever.

* When the time comes for you to leave your baby, make sure that you keep your goodbyes to a minimum. Be positive, use reassuring phrases and smile. Try giving a hug and kiss and a verbal reminder that you will be back soon.

Using the same approach and words each time you say goodbye will, in the long term, be more reassuring than going back to try and calm him down. While a baby will often cry when his mother or main carer leaves the room, he will be easy to distract in the hands of a competent carer. However babies are sensitive to moods, and if you are anxious and worried, your baby will pick up on this, and be more likely to get upset.

✿ Try to avoid 'just slipping away' when you leave your baby. Although you will find it difficult if he is upset when you say goodbye, it is much better for him to understand from you that you are going, and that you will return, than for you to slip away and your baby to look around and find you have vanished. This could contribute to his unhappiness – he might become confused, and clingy for fear of you just vanishing.

✿ Be realistic – you might well find that your baby is fretful at home even though the carer has told you that he is happy and content when you are not there. In the same way as you will find the change to your routine on your return to work tiring, so will your baby. Don't worry. Providing the circumstances are loving and secure, babies are adaptable.

✿ During this period of adjustment ask your baby's carer to ensure that your baby is not subjected to too many new experiences or for him to be handled by strangers. The calmer and more predictable his routine, the quicker he will get over his feelings of anxiety.

✿ If your baby is used to just being with you for the first six months, adapting to a more lively environment can be challenging. If you have chosen a childminder who looks after other children, or a nanny share, your baby will need to adapt to a more noisy, dynamic environment than he is used to. You can help your baby by arranging regular play dates with only a small group of the mothers and babies. This will be enjoyable for you and enable your baby to get used to the noise and activity of other children. If you have a nervous baby you will find that he will become happier once he is used to a different environment. Gradually introduce him into larger groups and other experiences. Generally babies love the activities of toddlers, so providing they are appropriately monitored, you can feel reassured that it will be a pleasant experience for him.

Stranger anxiety

At around six months you might find that your sociable baby is much more wary of strangers. This is a natural part of his development. It is thought that this 'fear of strangers' is a biological response relating to our origins. For a baby to survive in a primitive environment, a fear of strangers was not only a natural protective response but also contributed to their ability to survive.

We have an expectation that babies are happy to be handed to loving relatives and friends for cuddles when they are small, but even young babies can find being passed from one loving relative to the next, tiring and at times distressing.

- If your baby begins to cry when approached by strangers, or to look away when someone is trying to engage him, don't attempt to push him to communicate. It is much better to explain that your baby is becoming self-conscious and having a shy period, than to expect your baby to smile on cue!

- You can ease this response to those friends and family you see regularly by talking to your baby about them. If you have a photo montage on the wall, you can show your baby photographs and name the people in them. Role-play can help too. Give your baby's toys the names of the friends and family with whom you want him to be familiar.

- For close relatives or friends who see your baby frequently it can be upsetting when your child is distressed or tearful in response to them, but this usually passes once the person has been there for a while.

- Discourage people from making too much fuss of your baby when they first arrive. Sometimes a baby can find the physical proximity threatening. It is better if he is allowed to respond in his own time, once he feels comfortable with the person, than when someone is attempting to make eye contact, communicate and hold him.

✿ Although your baby will learn how to deal with greetings and attention as he grows up, some children remain shy. It is much better for you to adapt to this, and try to understand how it feels to be a shy child, than to push your child into situations where he feels uncomfortable or distressed.

6
Other Causes
of Crying

I have discussed many of the most common reasons that babies may cry, but there are some other issues that you could consider if you haven't been able to work out what is upsetting your baby. Some may seem obvious but they can be easily overlooked, so it is worth running through the list below if you have already been through all the other causes.

Nappy changing and nappy rash

It may sound obvious, but babies do sometimes cry when their nappies need changing because they are uncomfortable. It is always worth checking whether this is the cause of crying. If your baby's nappy is not changed frequently, he may get nappy rash which occurs when his delicate skin is in contact with the contents of a soiled nappy. It can also be caused by an infection or allergy. If you think this is the case you should consult a doctor.

Mild nappy rash is quite common and you may notice pink spots or blotches – these shouldn't cause too much discomfort. However, nappy rash can be quite severe with red, broken skin and painful swellings or blisters that cause your baby to cry a lot. In this condition, wash your baby's bottom with baby oil instead of water.

If your baby has mild nappy rash, try leaving his nappy off for a while every now and then. If you change him frequently and use a good barrier cream, the nappy rash should clear up within a few days. If your baby has severe nappy rash or nappy rash that won't go away, it is advisable to see your doctor.

Teething

Babies usually cut their first teeth between six and nine months, and it does not affect them all the same way. There are some common signs of teething to look out for:

* Red cheeks that may feel warm.

* More dribbling than usual.

* A rash around the mouth and chin.

* Red or swollen gums.

* Chewing everything he can get his hands on.

* Seeming restless and irritable.

If your baby gets grizzly or irritable when he is teething, try giving him a sachet of homeopathic teething powder or rubbing his gums with teething powder to ease the pain. You could also offer him one of the specially designed teething rings to chew on.

If your baby has a slightly reaised temperature or diarrhoea it is best that you contact your doctor rather than assume these symptoms are simply a sign of teething. In my experience, genuine teething pain can cause a few disruptive nights, but should not go on for several weeks. I have come across a number of cases where parents have put their baby's symptoms down to teething, when in fact he has what turns out to be an ear or throat infection.

Temperature

Newborn babies aren't good at regulating their body temperature and can suffer if they are too cold or too hot. This may cause them to cry. You should ensure that the temperature in your house is right for your baby, and that he is dressed appropriately for the weather.

* The ideal room temperature for your baby is about 18°C (64°F). An overheated room can be very uncomfortable for a baby.
* Avoid quilts, bumpers and pillows in your baby's cot as they can cause overheating.

- If you are swaddling your baby it is important to adjust the layers of bedding in the cot or Moses basket so that he doesn't overheat.

- Remember to reduce the layers of bedding on your baby's cot in hot weather.

- When the weather is very hot, pulling down the black-out blind may help to keep a room cool. You may also want to use a fan.

- In hot weather, your baby may be happy in just a nappy and T-shirt during the early part of the night.

- Layers of clothing are a good way to keep your baby warm if it is cold, as you can then take them off as appropriate.

- Don't forget a hat if you are taking your baby out in cold weather, and keep his feet and hands covered.

- Some young babies hate being undressed and will cry every time their clothes are changed. This may be partly to do with the fact that they lose body heat without their clothes on.

The Moro reflex

Also known as the 'startle reflex', the Moro reflex can be a cause of crying. Your young baby will throw back his arms in a startled, jumpy manner if he is alarmed by a sudden noise or if he feels as if he is falling. Your baby may then burst out crying. This is a perfectly normal phase of development which usually stops once a baby reaches four or five months. Swaddling a baby, or tucking him in securely, during sleep time will prevent the Moro reflex from waking him.

Comforters

Many babies like to have a comforter, whether it is a special toy or a blanket, and this often helps them to settle. However, think carefully before you introduce a comforter to your baby as you may have problems if you do this and he can't find it in the night.

Coughs and colds

Your baby may catch a cough or cold at some point during his first year. Young babies can get very distressed when they have colds, especially when they are trying to feed, as they will have blocked noses and cannot breathe well while sucking. You can try clearing mucus from his nose using saline drops and a suction bulb – but do not use the drops for more than two days without consulting a doctor. You can also use a cool mist vaporiser to moisten the air.

If your baby has been weaned, he may start to refuse solid food if he has a cold, and you may have to go back to giving him a milk feed in the night. It is important that he doesn't get dehydrated, so do make sure he gets plenty of liquid. Giving him a night feed should only be a temporary measure. If he does continue to wake up in the night once he is fully recovered, you can check on him and give him some cooled boiled water, but only if advised by your GP or health visitor. He will soon get back into his routine.

Your baby may cry if he is left to lie flat for too long when he has a cold. It may help to elevate his mattress slightly so that it is on a slope. If your baby has a high temperature and starts coughing a lot, or the mucus from his nose starts to look a greenish colour, you should seek medical advice as his cold could have developed into an infection.

Illness

Your baby will cry if he has an ear or throat infection, or is in any kind of pain. If he has a high temperature or fever, especially if it is accompanied by diarrhoea and sickness or any other symptoms, don't be afraid to seek medical advice sooner rather than later. Mothers are often worried that they may be seen as fussy or neurotic, but it is important to discuss any concerns you may have with your doctor. A sick baby will need peace, quiet and rest and it is a good idea to avoid too many visitors, especially in the evening, or too much activity. If your baby is ill, it is essential to follow your doctor's advice carefully, especially on feeding.

Wheeziness and allergies

Some babies do suffer with wheeziness and coughing, which can make them cry. You should see your doctor about this, but there are also some things that you can do to help. Make sure you air rooms by leaving the window open regularly (although don't do this when your baby is in the room if it is cold). Pay attention to how you wash bed linen, choosing a 60°C wash to eliminate house mite droppings. Ensure you do not have lots of stuffed toys near your baby's bed for this same reason.

Some babies have allergies or intolerances that can cause distress. It can sometimes be a reaction to something in their mother's milk. If you notice that your baby always seems upset after you have eaten a certain food, it is worth excluding it for a while and seeing if it makes a difference. Keep a food diary to see if you can spot any clear patterns emerging.

Bumps and bruises

Sometimes, your baby may cry because he has hurt himself. Young babies often bang themselves on the head with things they are trying to inspect, and once your baby becomes mobile, he is inevitably going to suffer some bumps and bruises. Babies who can sit sometimes topple over if they try to reach out, crawling babies can bang into things and when your baby is learning to walk he will fall now and again. These bumps and bruises are usually superficial and will quickly clear up but you should always seek medical advice to be sure. Try to remain calm when an accident happens; your baby may sense your panic and be more upset by your anxiety than his own injury.

Stages of development

Babies go through growth spurts during their first year, and these can be accompanied by unsettled phases when they cry more than usual. Try not to be unduly worried if your baby sometimes seems unsettled for a day or two, but do work your way through the possible causes in order to rule them out.

I truly believe that the most important thing you can do to help your baby and keep him happy is to follow a routine. If your baby's feeding and sleeping needs are being fully met, he is far more likely to be contented and far less likely to cry.

Conclusion

All babies will cry at times; some may cry loudly when they have their nappy changed or are being bathed, or perhaps when they hear a sudden loud noise. This type of crying I believe to be fairly normal and usually lasts for no more than a few minutes at a time. However, from my own personal experience of working with 300 babies and advising a further 6,000 parents through my consultancy service, I have found that if a baby is unsettled, and crying for lengthy periods of time, there is always an underlying cause.

In nearly all cases where I have had to deal with a baby who was crying excessively I found that structuring the baby's feeding and sleeping, and ensuring that the baby received the right balance of love and stimulation so that he did not become overtired or overstimulated, always resulted in a calm and contented baby. If you are struggling with a crying baby, by using all the advice and information in this book I

am confident you will soon be able to pin-point and eliminate all the possible causes, so that your baby goes from
being a crying baby to a contented baby.

Useful Resources

The Foundation for the Study of Infant Deaths (FSID)
Helpline: 0808 802 6868
www.fsid.org.uk

La Leche League
Tel: 0845 456 1855
www.laleche.org.uk

NCT (The National Childbirth Trust)
Tel: 0300 330 0770
www.nctpregnancyandbabycare.com

Sure Start
Tel: 08002 346 346
www.direct.gov.uk/surestart

Twins and Multiple Births Association (TAMBA)
Tel: 01483 304442
Twinline: 0800 138 0509
www.tamba.org.uk

Further Reading

A Contented House with Twins by Gina Ford and Alice Beer (Vermilion 2006)

Gina Ford's Top Tips for Contented Babies and Toddlers by Gina Ford (Vermilion 2006)

Feeding Made Easy by Gina Ford (Vermilion 2008)

Potty Training in One Week by Gina Ford (Vermilion 2003)

Silent Nights by Brian Symon (OUP Australia and New Zealand 2005)

Sleep: The Secret of Problem-free Nights by Beatrice Hollyer and Lucy Smith (Cassell 2002)

The Complete Sleep Guide for Contented Babies and Toddlers by Gina Ford (Vermilion 2006)

The Contented Baby with Toddler Book by Gina Ford (Vermilion 2009)

The Contented Baby's First Year by Gina Ford (Vermilion 2007)

The Contented Child's Food Bible by Gina Ford (Vermilion 2005)

The Contented Little Baby Book of Weaning by Gina Ford (Vermilion 2006)

The Contented Toddler Years by Gina Ford (Vermilion 2006)

The Gina Ford Baby and Toddler Cook Book by Gina Ford (Vermilion 2005)

The New Contented Little Baby Book by Gina Ford (Vermilion 2006)